First edition for the United States and Canada published
in 2006 by Barron's Educational Series, Inc.

First edition for Great Britain published
in 2006 by Hodder Children's Books

All inquiries should be addressed to:
Barron's Educational Series, Inc.
250 Wireless Boulevard
Hauppauge, New York 11788
www.barronseduc.com

Library of Congress Control Number: 2005934217

ISBN-13: 978-0-7641-3216-2
ISBN-10: 0-7641-3216-4

Printed in China
9 8 7 6 5 4 3 2 1

Disclaimer
The Web site addresses (URLs) included in this book were
valid at the time of going to press. However, because of
the nature of the Internet, it is possible that some addresses
may have changed, or sites may have changed or closed
down since publication. While the publisher regrets any
inconvenience this may cause readers, no responsibility for
any such changes will be accepted by the publisher.

Do I Have to Go to School?

A FIRST LOOK AT STARTING SCHOOL

PAT THOMAS
ILLUSTRATED BY LESLEY HARKER

You are about to go
on a big adventure.

You are going to see new things and learn new things and meet new people...and you will still be home in time to play before dinner.

The place you are going to is called a school.
Schools are where children go to learn new
things and make new friends.

Everyone feels a bit worried when they start school.

It's OK to wonder if you will like your teacher and
the other children and if you will be able to do all
the lessons and make new friends.

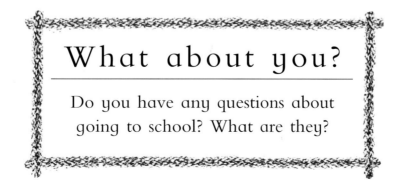

What about you?

Do you have any questions about
going to school? What are they?

It's also OK to wonder
why you have to go to
school at all.

After all, you have learned lots of new things from your family and have made some friends already.

School is a place where
you begin to learn about
the world outside of
your family...

...and the more you know about the world, the more interesting it becomes.

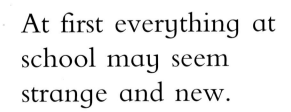

At first everything at
school may seem
strange and new.

You may not know where to find everything or who everyone is. It may seem a bit noisy and you may not feel like joining in.

But before you know it, your teacher will
be helping you to learn about numbers
and counting and how to write
your name and how plants
and animals grow.

Most of the time it may not even feel like learning. That's because teachers know lots of special ways to make learning fun.

What about you?

Can you think of some other fun things you could do in school?

At school there will be paints and crayons,
trains and blocks, dolls and cars,
and dressing-up boxes.

You will read stories and sing songs and dance...

and play outside and eat your lunch with lots
of other children.

Some things may change when you start school. You may have to get up a bit earlier each day to make sure you get to school on time, and you will see your parents less than you did before.

Once you are there, your parents won't be able to stay and play with you as they can at home. You may miss them.

But every day when you get home you will have lots to tell them about the things you did.

There will be some new rules to learn – like having to hang your coat up on a special peg...

or to sit quietly when your teacher is talking or reading to you.

But some rules will be just like the ones at home – like saying "please" and "thank you" and sharing your toys and not being unkind to others.

What about you?

Why do you think there are rules at school? Can you think of some other rules that might be the same at school and at home?

When you eat good food you get
all you need to help
your body grow
stronger.

When you learn new things you give your mind
what it needs to grow healthy and strong, too.

And when your body and
mind are healthy and
strong…

...you will have everything you need to grow into the special person you are meant to become.

HOW TO USE THIS BOOK

Going to school is a big change for everyone, but its greatest impact is on your child. Remember, small children don't have adult coping skills, so make sure your child gets extra attention and care at this time. School is just one of many new situations your child will have to face throughout his or her life. Adults can help children feel more secure by helping them to know what to expect. Consider the following points to help:

If you have encouraged your child's natural curiosity and a love of learning from the beginning, school is unlikely to be an overwhelming prospect. You can help your child love learning and take an interest in the world by taking advantage of everyday opportunities. Point out colors, shapes, animals, and numbers while out walking or traveling on the bus or in a car. Provide access to magazines, computers, and other learning tools. Regularly asking your child's opinion and including your child in family discussions will make the prospect of interacting with other adults less daunting.

The anxiety children feel about starting school is often not about school but about the unknown. Some of these unknowns include changes in an established routine, meeting new children, being treated as only one of many children, being away from a parent for a long time, dealing with new authority figures, and learning new rules. If you can, take your child to visit school before the term starts. Meet the teacher, see the classroom where your child will spend most of the day, and explore the playground. Anything like this will help lessen the fear of the unknown.

Even if your child doesn't express much concern about school, don't assume he or she is anxiety free. Not all children feel able to express their fears. Open-ended questions such as "Have you been thinking about what you will do at school?" can elicit useful answers and discussions. Expect mixed emotions even after your child has started school. Be sympathetic and ready to listen.

Try to associate school in your child's mind with things that are pleasurable. Emphasize all the fun things that go on in school. If your child is going to be with friends, get together with the other parents and their children and talk with the children about the good things they will experience at school. In addition, talk to your child about what happened in school each day – your interest may prove contagious.

Don't forget the practical aspects of starting school. Give yourself extra time in the morning so you are not rushing or panicking. Nobody likes to start the day this way. It is also important that your child has a good breakfast each day and provisions for a nutritious lunch while at school. And make sure your child gets enough sleep to avoid being tired and cranky at school.

BOOKS TO READ

First Day, Hooray!
by Nancy Poydar (Holiday House, 2000)

Miss Malarkey Doesn't Live in Room 10
by Judy Finchler and Kevin O'Malley (Walker Books for Young Readers, 1996)

The Night Before Kindergarten
by Natasha Wing and Julie Durrell (Grosset & Dunlop, 2001)

Welcome to Kindergarten
by Anne Rockwell (Walker Books for Young Readers, 2004)

RESOURCES FOR ADULTS

All About Moms
www.allaboutmoms.com
A Web site full of helpful advice and information for mothers of children of all ages. Find articles, information, resources, interactive tools, message forums, ask the experts, and more!

A Mom's Touch
www.amomstouch.com
A Web site containing advice on raising children at all stages. It includes general parenting issues, fun activities for kids, and more.

KidsGrowth.com
www.kidsgrowth.com
A Web site developed by pediatricians for parents. Contains information on children's health and growth issues, including a tremendous amount of information on various aspects of schooling.

The United Federation of Teachers (UFT)
Headquarters:
52 Broadway
New York, NY 10004
212-777-7500
www.uft.org
Known for being a strong teachers' union in New York City, this organization maintains a Web site with information of value to all parents, dealing with a wide variety of school issues.

National Education Association (NEA)
Headquarters:
1201 16th Street, NW
Washington, DC 20036-3290
(202) 833-4000; Fax: (202) 822-7974
www.nea.org
The NEA believes that when parents are involved in their children's education, kids do better in school. In addition to the variety of resources their Web site provides, they have available two new parent guides to help ease the preschooler's transition to kindergarten and provide a checklist of baseline skills for school readiness.